JOSEPH WARREN BEACH

Beginning with Plato

POEMS

THE UNIVERSITY OF MINNESOTA PRESS
Minneapolis

Copyright 1944 by the
UNIVERSITY OF MINNESOTA

All rights reserved. No part of this book may be reproduced in any form without the written permission of the publisher. Permission is hereby granted to reviewers to quote brief passages in a review to be printed in a magazine or newspaper.

Printed at the Lund Press, Inc., Minneapolis

1 0

Contents

BEGINNING WITH PLATO, 1943-1944 1
TO AN ANCIENT SORCERER, 1. TO MYSELF, 4. TO A MODERN METAPHYSICAL POET, 6. HISTORY LESSON, 9. STRATEGOS, 19. THE UNIFORM, 21. THE HEAVENLY BIRD, 23. CRAZY BARQUE, 25. FOR ME THE ANSWER, 26. MOTTO FOR TOLSTOI'S "WAR AND PEACE," 29. TO THE POET OF FAUST, 30. TO SEE A WORLD IN A GRAIN OF SAND, 31. UNDERGROUND, 32. PERSONAL DIALECTIC, 33. SIGHT UNSEEN, 35.

CYPRIAN HYMN, 1927 37

FROM THE WEST, 1920 42
CANTICLE, 42. THE LONELY BUILDER, 44. THE MILK OF THE DESERT, 45. HIBISCUS, 46. THE HIGH MOUNTAINS, 47.

THE LIFE WE IMAGE 53
LIVING ROOM, 53. WINTER NIGHT, 54. PERENNIAL, 55. SWAN MAIDEN, 56. BLOOD IS THICKER THAN WATER, 57. AFFINITIES, 58. CAVE TALK, 59. THE VIEW AT GUNDERSON'S, 61. THE DANCE IN THE STEERAGE, 62. SWANHILD, 63. SUCCESS STORY, 64. SALUTE, 65. LOVE IN AMBUSH, 66. CHRISTMAS TREES, 67. THE BLACK LAND, 68. SUCCESSION, 69. THE RED LAND, 70. SONGS FOR DAGMAR, 71.

MINNEAPOLIS SKYLINES, 1915 73
THE CHIMNEYS, 73. POWER, 74. MILWAUKEE DEPOT, 75. BOHEMIAN FLATS, 76. URBAN COLLOQUY, 77.

PARISIAN DRYPOINTS, 1913 78
PONT ROYAL, 78. QUAI VOLTAIRE, 80. RUE DE SEINE, 81. SAINT GERMAIN DES PRÉS, 82. FOLIES-BERGÈRE, 83. CAFÉ D'HARCOURT, 84. CAFÉ STEINBACH, 85. BOULEVARD CLICHY, 86. RUE BONAPARTE, 87. PARC MONCEAU, 88. QUAI D'ORSAY, 89.

ACKNOWLEDGMENTS 92

BEGINNING WITH PLATO
1943-1944

To an Ancient Sorcerer

Sweet master of ventriloquists
Who with the voice of Socrates
Have laid us under such a spell
As holds us bound though ill at ease,

You never put the least constraint
Upon the tenderest neophyte,
But gently by the painless paths
Of reason lead him to the light.

Ah, tolerant of myth and fable
That shadow forth eternal Forms
But down on any little facts
That overstrain the sacred norms!

It would be disingenuous
And smacking even of presumption
To doubt your least conclusion once
We grant your primary assumption.

How sadly and reluctantly
We're brought to question your award!
But instincts deep and primitive
Admonish us to be on guard

Lest with the silken cords you've drawn
Out of ourselves you subtly bind
And swaddle up our infant limbs
And even the movements of the mind.

And first we question whence you fetch
Those prime abstractions that precede,
Anticipate and quite fill up
The smallest items of your creed.

We fear to trust our thoughts so far
Beyond the bounds of deed and sense
We cannot bring them to the test
Of feeling and experience.

But most, sweet master, underneath
Your exquisite humility
We dread your self-assurance as
A menace to our liberty.

You are so well at ease yourself
In Zion — that's eternity —
Your model state's a puritan
Philosopher's autocracy.

And we that grope and search and climb
Along the dark and rugged steep,
Your plan is sure to lap us soft
And warm in one eternal sleep.

You that have purged the Olympian gods
Of errors from the West and East
Would turn the sceptic over to
The tender mercies of the priest.

The cobbler and the carpenter
You would exclude from rule and rank
And find your liberal masters . . . well . . .
Cutting coupons in the bank?

We've seen how things work out. The state
Transcendent draws distinctly nearer,
A blacksmith for a Duce, and
A paper hanger for a Fuehrer.

To Myself

Concerning Plato, dearest heart,
And many another saint and sage,
You have unloosed a spate of words
Unworthy of considered age,

Forgetful in your callow zeal
That it is little short of treason
To take your stand with those who doubt
The rule of holiness and reason.

The half-truths you have fathered in
A flush of intellectual pride
Seem falsehoods pure and simple when
Regarded from the other side.

Take Plato, whom you have arraigned
For underhand conspiracy
Against the rights of man and mind's
Inalienable sovereignty,

Brave Plato! throwing overboard
Without regret habit, convention,
Party and prejudice as things
Almost too frivolous for mention,

And sailing blithely forward over
Waters treacherous and uncouth
With never a mark to guide him but
The star of dialectic truth.

Uncanny mariner! but you
Would surely not prefer to share
Your passage with those mutinous
Buccaneers of laissez-faire!

You wish your saints within the will
Of man would sprout self-rising leaven
Sufficient for the bread of life
And not in some unlikely heaven.

You wish that Plato'd had a touch
Of Claude Bernard and Francis Bacon,
A notion of the role of facts
In proving theories mistaken.

But ah! confess you'd rather be
Doorkeeper in the house of myth
Than dwell forever in the tents
Of Edison and Adam Smith.

Confess, poor fool, and make it heard
Distinctly in and out of season,
You stand with those who never doubt
The rule of holiness and reason.

To a Modern Metaphysical Poet

I

The devil is in it,
The war you wage
On all that's substance
And form to an age.

Ages you scorn
As the issue of time
Lapsing fast to the vast
Aboriginal slime.

The root's in the dirt,
The flower's in thin air,
A worm's in the womb
Of the gravid pear.

Matter is muck,
Motion's impure,
Desire is a bawd
And spirit's a lure.

Freedom's licence,
Brotherhood
Is bird and baboon's
Call of blood.

Works are not faith
And faith is not works.
In word and act
Damnation lurks.

The ear denies
Whatever's heard.
You crave a soundless
Shapeless word

Beyond achievement
And perdition,
Understanding,
Definition.

Outside the world,
Beyond the law,
You bake eternal
Bricks without straw.

So on empty
Wind and sighs
Feeds the worm
That never dies.

II

You, with your absolutes!
Where did you find 'em?
Turning plain men to brutes . . .
And why do you mind 'em?

Drugged through the sunshine,
Riding all night
In an old bawdy charnel house
Figures of fright,

What ghost has whispered
Being no god
You're but a death's-head
This side the sod?

This side the sod
Bloom like a flower
Letting eternity
Fill up the hour!

Words are but spooks
You've made up yourself.
Time those old ghosts were laid
And laid on the shelf.

Bad is not-good, and good's
All to the good.
That's true arithmetic
For the quick blood.

All that you've missed
Is gone to the devil.
To all that you've made
Do learn to be civil!

History Lesson

I

It was an ill wind brought them down
In Shangri-La with flying gear
So badly knocked about they could
Not hope to sail in half a year.

The local priesthood without question
Gave them hearty cheer and pardon
And left them to disport themselves
At will in their enchanted garden.

But soon as they were tired of pacing
And musing there in cloistered ease,
Mr. Hull got out his Bible
And Eden his Thucydides.

Not that they hoped in such a fix
To take much solid satisfaction
In reading ancient chronicles —
These grounded modern men of action.

But Mr. Hull was taught to think
The Holy Bible held the clue
To virtue, and had always meant
To take the time to read it through,

And Mr. Eden had been trained
To think the sacred mystery
Of statesmanship was best enshrined
In Greek and ancient history.

So there they sat in high Tibet
With spectacles upon their noses
And puckered brows the while the bees
Hummed drowsily among the roses.

And Mr. Hull in Shangri-La,
Now by a world at war forgotten,
Ploughed steadily through chronicles
Of who was who, by whom begotten,

While Mr. Eden learned the names
Of those who stood against the Sophy,
Returned the bodies under truce
Hellenic, and set up a trophy.

At length the British statesman yawned.
"Well, friend," said he, "what do you find
In Hebrew scripture to support
The spirit and inform the mind?"

"I find," said Mr. Hull, "and here
I'm sure all liberals will agree,
That Moses followed in his wars
An unenlightened policy,

"Being, as we must think today,
No proper mouthpiece of the Lord
When he required his captains to
Put women and children to the sword.

"He'd far too little to my taste
Of knightly Oliver and Roland,
And far too much of Nazi ways
These days in Russia and in Poland."

"No doubt," said Mr. Eden, "more
Of Christian spirit will be found
Within the gospels." "Yes," said Hull,
And glanced uneasily around,

"One must confess the gospels teach
A doctrine beautiful and mystic.
But don't you find in state affairs
The golden rule . . . unrealistic?"

"Perhaps you're right. The other cheek . . .
Appeasement practised on a Punic
Adversary . . . Neville and Winston
Learned something at Madrid and Munich."

II

"But you, my friend," said Mr. Hull,
"What have you come across to please
And guide a statesman in the book
Of classical Thucydides?"

"How little Greece like David downed
The giant Median chivalry
At Salamis and Marathon,
Plataea and Thermopylae,

"While Hellas and the islands raised
To Grecian gods exultant paeans
For having saved the goodly soil
Of Europe for the Europeans."

"Ah, there!" said Mr. Hull, and both
Were gravely silent for a spell,
Reflecting proudly, earnestly,
Upon a modern parallel.

"So Athens made herself the head
Of a far-flung confederacy,"
Said Eden, "plighted to the end
Of keeping land and ocean free."

"Oh, good!" said Mr. Hull. "And then,"
Said Eden, "comes the golden age
For Athens, when the liberal arts
Are acted out as on a stage

"For all the world, when justice holds
Her balance even, and at their ease
All men within the law can think
And do exactly as they please."

"Amen!" said Mr. Hull. "And yet
This admirable democracy,
As I have heard, was founded on
A base of chattel slavery,

"A thought which no American
Can stomach." Eden made a mouth.
"I did not think," he said, "that you
Were so particular in the South."

"The South!" cried Hull. "Why don't you stick
To subjects in your competence?"
"*Touché!*" said Eden, "I will try
Hereafter to show better sense."

"My fault," said Hull. "Pray be assured
I'd no idea of offending.
Go on with Greece. I do so hope
The story has a happy ending."

III

"Well, not so happy. And what's more,
It's difficult to find the reason.
Some dry rot must have started at
The height of Athens' flowering season.

"You see, for Athens empire was
An absolute necessity
For keeping what she had — her trade,
Dominion, and hegemony.

"She'd grown so great — like Britain — she
Could not maintain her liberties
Nor even feed her slaves without
Unchallenged mastery of the seas.

"But those her colonies and states,
Allies and kingdoms tributary
Were jealous of her dominance
And backward in their payments — very!

"Then Sparta, Corinth, Argos, and
The small fry of the Peloponnese
Banded together to dispute
The imperial sovereignty of Greece.

"Now, Sparta was — of course you know —
The model oligarchic state —
Fascist we'd call it, everything
In short that you and I would hate."

"Of course," said Hull. "Our record long
Has made our deep abhorrence plain
For dictators in every form
In France and Italy and Spain."

"But fascists have their qualities,
Among which one might underscore
Firmness in peace, efficiency
Both in diplomacy and war.

"Their shrewdest trick was to foment
Intrigues among the upper classes
Eager to sell the state and then
Take out their grudges on the masses."

"That has a modern sound," said Hull.
Said Eden, "Yes. In Athens' self
The plutocrats were quite prepared
To lay their empire on the shelf

"And call the Spartans in, so they
Might keep the rule. 'Twas merest chance
That Athens did not parallel
In every point the fate of France.

"Meantime the fighting fiercer raged
And farther like an epidemic
In spite of best diplomacy,
Intrigue, betrayal, and polemic,

"For thirty years. The blood of Greece
Was spilt upon the barren sods,
Coined silver spent and even the gold
Appropriated to the gods.

"The exploits of Demosthenes,
Pericles, Brasidas, Lysander,
Only made Greece an easier prey
To Philip and young Alexander."

IV

Then Mr. Hull and Mr. Eden
Within their lonely isle of peace
Mused silently and mournfully
Upon the glory that was Greece.

V

But Hull at length recovered force
To throw off his despondency.
"Was there no mention anywhere
Of right and reciprocity?"

"From time to time Thucydides
Adverts a trifle wistfully
To general laws that are the hope
Of weakness in adversity.

"It was to these the Melians
Appealed. But the Athenians,
Who wanted Melos, treated them
Like uninstructed Fenians.

"They reasoned with the islanders
In manner patient and urbane,
And showed them under Athens' rule
How much both parties stood to gain.

"'But as for right and justice, these
Come first in question among equals,
Whereas with powers inferior
Rights are determined by their sequels,

"'Since by the necessary laws
Of nature, be it for god or man,
The strong must needs be strong and strive
To rule the weaker where he can.'

"Melos stood firm. Athens reduced
The town by siege. The males they slew,
The women and children sold for slaves,
And colonized the town anew."

Hull sighed. "My undersecretaries
Opine that wars will rage so long
As justice does not hold the scales
Equal between the weak and strong.

"That's the right principle. But then
I fear it would be hard to rouse
Enthusiasm for its practice in
Either the Senate or the House.

"If one could only figure out
Some way to make the nations pool
Their interests and so give legal
Standing to the golden rule!"

VI

"Justice," said Eden, "is a flower
More fair than anything we know,
Late blooming on a sturdy stock
Of growth, alas! exceeding slow.

"First in the family and clan
  The seed takes root. But what a pity
  It is so very loth to spread
  Beyond the parish and the city!

"The glory of Greece is chiefly this,
  They first devoted earnest thought
  To right and law — their tragedy
  That all their labor came to nought.

"In many an armistice and treaty
  They used their best abilities
  To regulate disputes by law
  Without renewed hostilities.

"But honor, which within the tribe
  Was virtue's crown from man to man,
  Was turned to double-dealing and
  Blood-letting between clan and clan.

"Yet in the end, I fancy, what
  They dreamed of right throughout the ages
  Has had more power in the world
  Than all their treacheries and rages.

"What is most precious, man has found,
  Is ever the most hardly earned,
  And of all lessons justice is,
  It seems, the latest to be learned.

"So for the statesman what is needed
  Most is patience after skill."
"I should say faith," said Mr. Hull.
"I should say good faith and good will."

VII

So for a spell in Shangri-La
These earnest statesmen took their ease
And made their commentaries on
The Bible and Thucydides.

At length replacements came, and as
They were assured the plane would go,
Said Hull, "I trust no harm has come
To Franco or Badoglio!"

"Amen!" said Eden as he stepped
Aboard and buttoned up his coat.
"The first rule for the statesman is:
In danger never rock the boat."

Strategos

Aristocrat by mind and birth
He put the honor of the state
Before the jealous pride of class
And earned the Better People's hate.

His navies sailed the farthest seas,
Trade flourished like the green bay tree,
And unemployment was absorbed
In peristyle and metope.

His measured eloquence and calm
Forensic made the classes squirm.
The masses found that he made sense
And chose him leader term by term.

But when the envious factions fell
Like wolves upon the magistrate
A popular assembly broke
The pillar of the people's state. . . .

Let this be Athens in the days
Of Phidias, Euripides,
Piraeus and the Parthenon,
And call the statesman Pericles. . . .

Give him a limp . . . for mastery
Over the first and worst of foes . . .
A saucy cigarette advanced
Before a fine patrician nose.

In place of Periclean dome
Give him a firm protruding chin
For catching wisecracks as they come
With wiser crack and deadlier grin . . .

In Wall Street now the oligarchs
Endure with blood and sweat and tears
More than a decade. Pericles
Kept the lead for thirty years. . . .

Oh, ship the young men overseas
In navy blouse and khaki coat,
And count the ballots in the bank —
But never count the soldier vote!

The Uniform

I

The child sleeps, or more likely keeps
His eyes shut fast against the light,
Lips pursed. The soldier holds him
A trifle awkwardly but tight—

No, firmly and responsibly—
And gazes on him with an air
That seems to question how an armful
So unaccustomed settled there

Upon his breast. The uniform
And shoulder straps as in surprise
At such employment hold them stiff.
The infant unprotesting lies.

He lets himself be held. He knows
Instinctively his part for years
Is simply to be nourished, guarded
Somehow against his pains and fears.

II

This khaki, though he wears it well,
Is foreign to the young man still.
He was not born to crush and maim
Or to beat down another's will.

He was most manifestly born
To cherish life and let it flower.
But fire must be fought with fire,
And hell's the password to this hour.

Until the hour strikes he may hold
His rainbowed future to his heart—
Not long, but long enough to scan
And memorize a soldier's part.

The uniform, the token bars
That hold the muscled shoulders straight
Are more than courage, more than will,
And something else than blood and hate.

The cradled infant lets him know
His calling. And his shadowed face
Gravely reflects and holds in trust
The budding promise of his race.

The Heavenly Bird

Who's there? *An angel.* Angel? *Ay,
Spirit.* But that is me! *A bird
Of flaming wings, have you not heard,
Beyond these mortal haunts to fly.*

Beyond? *Away, without, above!*
O bird, it must be passing strange
In such a blank abyss to range
Beyond the touch of all we love!

*Beyond the touch of sin! Without
The evil beating of the blood.*
Why then, without the pulse of good
And all our striving brings about!

*Nay, at the origin and springs
Of good, from earth withdrawn, apart.*
I only know that in my heart
The living water boils and sings.

Alas, poor child! The fluting fails,
The vision dwindles to a wraith.
O fickle bird! *O child of death,
Know it is faith alone prevails*

With all that baffles eye and ear.
Faith? faith? A glancing thought reveals
What the dull moment ill conceals
Of past and future, far and near.

What have the feathers from the blue
To show me that I do not know?
*The sleeping soul I come to show
How from the false to wake the true.*

The heavenly truth incessantly
Sleeps on the mirror of the heart,
And will is eager, for his part,
To make the dream reality.

*And is the child grown man? The air
Is steep and blank.* Sweet heavenly bird,
I harken but no voice is heard.
The airy plumes are vanished . . . where?

*Where runs the rainbow, man? My part
Is played and yours begun. The chill
Of heaven melts. . . . Make sure the will
Performs the bidding of the heart!*

Crazy Barque

This crazy barque that I have built
For cruising among the islands, caught
Now in the black fury that beats
Incessant down the shoreless main. . . .

All I have dreamed in feckless mood,
All I have started and let drop,
Tugs at the sails and crowds the keel
And puts the timbers on a strain,

Fair weather planks that warp and start
Under their paint being all that lies
Between me and the bitter drench
That puts to sleep the beating brain.

Night or day I cannot leave
The helm an instant, but just to keep
The old ramshackle right side up
Fight the seas with might and main,

Keep the course laid out for me
By all the powers that meet in one,
Will and ought and must and can,
Love and hate and loss and gain.

And you, unhandy skiff, must serve
To keep my precious cargo dry
So long as heart beats and hand
Does the bidding of the brain.

For Me the Answer

(TO R. P. W. AND A. C.)

Whatever storms may rage in secret deeps
Or tides may drive them toward what destinies —
These two — seeing that a wind of the spirit sweeps
Across the surface of the mysteries,

And spirit to spirit along the surface speaks
Explicitly as friendship may require,
Which mere exchange of understanding seeks
As fuel sufficient for the sacred fire. . . .

Here discourse is incessant questioning
Of worlds and men, a play supremely good
Since word is here identical with thing
And least intention swiftest understood.

I know not by what most unlikely chance
Such a community of tongues was born
That comprehension wakens at a glance
Instead of dead indifference and scorn —

Such a community of reference
As if our eyes from the beginning had dwelt
On the same objects, the same skies, and hence
With the same syllables the same meanings spelt.

Though diverse storms may rage in alien deeps
And drive us upon unlike destinies,
Across the surface of the one sea sweeps
And wakes our hearts and tongues the one salt breeze,

And wakes our questioning of men and things.—
You, Dante fallen on bewildered days,
I have no quarrel with you, though bitter springs
Turn your best praise of man's life to dispraise.

You have hung your stars so far beyond the reach
Of men like us who cling to broken spars. . . .
But there is never a doubt that on the beach
Of heaven are strewn for you authentic stars.

And you, young Plato, from the pure serene
Of dialectic reason where you dwell,
Know all too clear what facts and records mean
Not to have felt the searing breath of hell.

Your certainty of truth is tentative
As Dante's of untruth, and so together
You keep the windy argument alive
That makes you glamorous two birds of a feather.

The sudden shift of scenes as one breaks through
To new dimensions of the exploring mind—
The catch of breath, and yet assurance too
One need not fear with these to go it blind. . . .

The oracle is dark and little enough
Of all your splendor through the stammering shines,
And in the end iambics leave the stuff
Of the spirit to be read between the lines.

Perhaps in the end friendship is wave-lengths tuned
So nicely that with the least of fuss and fret
What in your sending-set is whispered, crooned,
Comes out most clear from my receiving-set.

That sure is perfect luck, and that, my sage,
Whether in assertion or in questioning,
Is what upon this present happy stage
Of being makes a person of a thing.

The while you put the questions, friends, for me
You are the answer living and complete.
How to sum up time and eternity
So as most sure the devil to defeat?

Eternity defines the possible
In time, and time from out that vacant blue
Has drawn for me no facts material,
My friends, nor truths definitive as you.

Motto for Tolstoi's "War and Peace"

He that is good and loves not goodness
Bakes no bread for any soul.
He that loves good, though he destroy it,
What he breaks he shall make whole.

She that loves not casts no shadow.
She that loves, though she be long
Lost, by love's magic shall redeem
What gardens unto love belong.

Son of man must sink to hell
And grope the ways from light withdrawn
Before his mortal eyes can taste
The flush and healing of the dawn.

To the Poet of Faust

All the heart most finely
Breathes, but the envious tongue
Cheapens, is the candid
Burden of your song.

Horrors that the craven
With averted glance
Shuns, you seize and freeze in
Deathless witches' dance.

Braveries by time
Bedeviled, fouled and broken
Raise from the dust and hallow
With right word found and spoken!

To See a World in a Grain of Sand

He steeps the wild anemones
In blown Venetian glass. His foot
Is light on webs of Iran spread
With ritual vine and cone and flower.

His eyes beyond his arbor rest
On melting blues closing a scene
Flawless in charm as aught Giorgione's
Self conceived . . . Ah, well-a-day!

Jesting Pilate shrank the world
Into a speck of bitter dust,
And honor sold will bleach the heaven
Out of each last anemone.

Underground

(FOR RUTH AND PAUL)

When the republic betrays, when the capitol
Turns bedlam, when the White House melts
Like metal in the heat, and from treetop to treetop
Over islanded seas the spider spreads his blight,

When the only blossoms that show are monsters —
Mosleys, Francos, Goebbels, Lavals —
And the leaves fall in a rain of blood,
While Mammon readjusts his verminous ermine,

When the winds are foul and the sun chills . . .
The sap convulsed returns on itself
Underground, to the shrinking roots,
The darkling, sheltering, burrowing roots,

Where man's will sleeps and gathers strength.
Do they think that Jefferson's dead, or Christ?
Do they think no drive is left to the dream
Of Milton, Rousseau, Lenin, Garibaldi?

When trees fall without stroke of the ax,
Leafless majesty crumbling to dust,
Green from the roots over all the islands
Sprouts renewed the unbetraying republic.

Personal Dialectic

Be still for once and let the moment
Rest in the palm of your spirit, resting
For once, accepting and possessing
This hour of April turning May —

These cloudy fringes of a protoplasmic
Tide released along the balanced
Vaulting stems of thorn and elm —
This piercing of the sand, this sudden

Apparition of the crocus
Heralded by the meadowlark
In the freshness of suspended showers —
This captivating, most undeniable

Moment of all the calendar
Denied again! O most unbending
Of spirits, to your own good opposed —
O palsied clutching fingers that never,

Never close on the proffered gift,
The timeless hour! What shadow of bliss
So drives you toward what bleak November,
Heaped granary and heart unfilled?

April stays not, not for an instant.
The eye fails, but the leafbuds swell,
The laces thicken, and the treetops
Momently shut out more sky.

*It is the plunging heart's illusion
That makes this breathless tender moment
Of recollection and surrender,
This offer of timelessness and rest.*

*Nothing in all the calendar
Holds, there is nought but forward straining
Passage from now-then to thereafter,
And life is not in the resting form,*

*But the moving line, the tracing curve.
I that am life live not in timeless
Instants but in the straining passage
From what I am to what I would be.*

The head is clear but the heart is void,
The heart is weary of completion
Never complete. The heart craves rest
Of recollection and surrender.

You — if you cannot hold the moment
Simply, cannot cease from striving —
Strive to catch the timeless hour
In the net of words, of straining words.

Shadow in words the protoplasmic
Tide released, the thickening leafbuds
Momently screening off the sky,
The blackbird and the meadowlark

Between the scented showers saluting
The apparition of the crocus.
Let pride of being serve at length
The famished craving of the heart.

Sight Unseen

The hyacinths in the bowl are really
Flowers in vision — flushed whorls,
And bowl, and table, and that corner of the room
Lodged in my sight, and flowering there.

Pink clusters strewn with indigo —
Indigo flowrets cutting the sweet
Abandoned riot of the coral —
Slim dark stems among the blond,

Water-plumped and crisp and fleshy
Stems of the coral-tinted flowers —
Pale green bowl, black table-top,
And corner of the room in the eyes' vision.

Along the fence in the village yard
Before the maples are leaved in Missouri
Tossing their heads in the gray borders
She cut them quick before the snow fell.

But none of that is in the vision —
The eyes' vision — *Aunt Lucy by the fence*
Working fast in an April chill
While the first flakes aimlessly drift.

That's in the letter — or through the letter —
Mind's picture of April Macon
Never seen, telescoping with
Mind's picture of Macon August.

Black stove and cool porch,
Footsteps on the shadowed sidewalk,
Parched lawn, but safe enclosure
Against a world of screaming ghosts.

(Aunt Lucy's books echo the tale
Of how the young man's blood was shed,
Her borders show the hyacinthine
Resurrection of his manhood.

She knows what god with careless aim
Quenched his fire, and what a price
Apollo paid, the world pays,
For its most true and flowery legend.

She knows, but does not shape her knowledge.
Her wisdom hoards the end result,
The residue of blood and madness,
Foaming along the April fence.)

The hyacinths in the bowl are really
Flowers in the eyes' vision, and these —
Sweet fleshy scent and riot of curls —
Telescope with the mind's picture,

Double exposure, triple, multiple,
Film within film, life behind life,
Heart's ache, heart's balm,
Tensed spirit's leap to joy —

Heaped in this bowl in a corner of the room
Drinking the water with blond and fleshy
Stems and delicate tossing heads,
Sensed before seen as we come in,

Known here now to sight and smell
For half a week, and known as truly
It may be, to the mind's vision,
Heart's sight, for as long as we stay.

CYPRIAN HYMN
1927

Cyprian Hymn

Safe in the courts of love we have forgotten — the sunny courts of love set round with cedars — we have forgotten the pits of shame, the dismal swamps, dead trees with scaling bark and deadly vines, close-clinging, trailing slime . . . O wonder! O praised be Venus that we should ever have come through, past sights that freeze the blood like fearful dreams, dreams that beset the helpless spirit to sleep abandoned. Praised be Love!

There by his mottled pool Narcissus lies the prey of obscene birds, Narcissus, who so long time, deaf to the tender invitations of woodland girls, sealed up within the circle of his own passion, beseeching himself for love, for mercy, bloodless, haggard with incessant craving, was made the victim of his own image. His image, green from the mantled pool, rose like a wraith of mist from the stagnant water, and like a serpent round his throat and loins, strangled Narcissus. . . . How could we ever pass a sight so fearful? Praised be Venus!

How did we escape pollution of harpies, filthy birds with throats insatiable, forever swooping and snatching filth? Or those caged apes that torture one another and mishandle, or crouch alone in the gloom, passive and melancholy on their haunches? How did we escape the trampling of centaurs, herds of centaurs male and female, stampeding, spattering mud from frantic hooves, and straining to sever human breasts and shoulders from loins of beastly mare and stallion? Praised be Venus!

Here in the courts of love set round with cedars, poplar and maple spring in mounded spires, and oaks tough-fibred, branches firm-set in trunks millennial, down shameless aisles of woodland cast the shadow of their green fulfilment. Gravelled ways through grassy borders lead down by terraced gardens, by unexhausted fountains tossing rainbowed spray. And marble urns at measured intervals offer to Love oblation of purple flowers and the incense of flowers.

Round about the temple — set on the greenest hill, pillar and pediment of yellow marble veined with purple and rose — the Graces scatter the dew of the lawns with rose-veined feet, and there by light of the rising moon young Hyacinths unharmed play with the nymphs at discus-throwing. Unharmed Actaeon gazes on bathing Artemis. Leaving her tunic, leaving her bow and arrows and her maidens, she runs inviting down the leafiest track. Happy Actaeon! No fear of spotted hide and branching horns! You shall come on human feet with a man's hands to scatter incense on the sacred flame!

O praised be Venus, we have come through the place of tombs, the lurid desert without moon, without a star!

Our dragging feet we have freed from the sticky meshes of that nightmare. We could not move, we could not turn our eyes, when we beheld the son of Laius caught in the clutch of that riddling monster, half woman, half wildcat, stony haunches spreading backward in the dark clamped to the rock, the coffin-cover. Woman's breasts gleaming in the red light shed from a woman's eyes — her mother's eyes beaming with tender light, her mother's lips glued to his writhing bloodless lips. Soon he will lie beside his father beneath the rock, beneath those stony haunches. . . . Praised be Venus! we have forgotten. We have forgotten for we looked on Oedipus and knew him.

There in that lurid night we have seen men running, running in terror and glancing backward at men with knives pursuing. They were distorted shadows of themselves. And women terror-stricken, haunted with voices, haunted with shapes and voices, apes and parrots, whispering, shouting, offering, and accusing. These were their own cravings, severed fragments of self disowned, strangled and buried, returning livid from the tomb, the dead demanding to be reunited with the living. Ah seldom shall any, by grace of Love knowing herself, win through and find her peace within these sunny courts set round with cedars!

O blackest night behind the stony hill of Golgotha, bristling with spikes and sabres and lighted only with pallid and with blood-dripping blossoms of the cactus! There upon blasted cypress boles pale Christs hang agonizing, passionately submissive and beseeching imaginary legionaries to drive their nails through feet and hands. O self-accusing, self-exalting, these know not Venus, but with blood and gall, with thorns and spikes crucifying the flesh, they have raised themselves to godhead; they hang exalted above a world shuddering and terror-stricken.

Sadder than these, most sad and death-distilling, the tranced and lotos-bearing Buddhas, impotent, each in his gilded shrine, his gilded smile snake-like playing about his thin and sensual lips. Lovers of self and self-sufficient, in vain for them the temple-bells, dropping like lotos-petals through the air, measure the hours for those that labor in the rice-fields. In vain for them the pilgrims winding upward make the ascent of the holy mountain. In vain the sunlight prints on earth the image of the pine-branch, the moon follows the sun across the airy vault, and lovers together bathe in the moonlight as in holy water. Self-enchanted these are transported to a land where all is nothing.

We have known these horrors. We have been Narcissus and gazed despairingly on our own image. We have been Oedipus. We have chattered with apes and spattered mud in the mad stampede of centaurs. We have hung upon the blasted cypress and cried out for nails in hands and feet. We have folded hands and felt the gilded smile crawl round our lips, while the sun faded and the temple bells grew faint and ceased upon our ears stopped up. O praised be Venus! we have known ourselves and, knowing, we have freed our feet from the meshes of that nightmare. And now with feet unfettered we scatter dew of the lawns before the rose-veined temple. In the courts of love we have carved stone and raised up pillars. We have set words to the lyre and sung them, in Dorian mode and Lydian. We have known love and the fruits of love weigh down our boughs like golden apples. Praised be Love!

But last we paused beside that still and starless water, grown round with willows black and lustreless — that water, not water, that sticky, pallid, and repulsive fluid — drippings and drainings of wasted strength — that dim gray sheet of lake where in the center rises an isle funereal. Steep black rocks encircling a grove of cypress, at whose feet by the water's edge dim portals open inward to the cavernous heart of the rock. Are these the gates from which at birth we issued, that like a magnet draw desperate men across the lake of death, before their time, like desperate children, to crawl back in their mother's womb? One such we saw, shining in dead white cerements and rigid, floating in his black barque, a shape of death, having already paid the final price for peace.

We dared not linger, we dared not gaze, but dragged our feet through mud and slime from that shore bewitched, and ran like mad, sweating and shivering, until we reached the courts set round with cedars, where men and women sing together and dance in the sunlight, having forgotten the pits of shame, the dismal swamps, the place of tombs, the lake of death, knowing themselves at last and knowing Love. Oh, praised be Love!

FROM THE WEST
1920

Canticle

My belovèd and I shall meet
   in the heat of the day
   in the brooding shadows
   of the untrimmed orange trees,

And we shall walk together
   before night falls
   between the palm trees
   over against the mountains.

The lips of my belovèd are sweet
   as the juice of the orange
   falling at a touch
   from a branch long sunned,

And her words have something
   strong and bitter
   as the orange rind
   her teeth have bitten apart.

The dreams of my belovèd
   are the shadows of palms
   drowsily stirring
   on the brown adobe wall.

Her thoughts are large as the fronds
   of date palms in a row
   moving all together
   and shedding light from numberless blades.

Whoever has seen her in anger
   has beheld the tropical storm —
   proud branches twisting and writhing
   against a rain-swept sky. . . .

My belovèd and I shall meet
   in the heat of the day
   in the brooding shadows
   of the untrimmed orange trees,

And we shall walk together
   before night falls
   between the palm trees
   over against the mountains.

The Lonely Builder

I have built a home for my belovèd
Down a canyon neighboring the sky and the sea
Where the air is keen with smell of salt and sagebrush
And only wild things nest and burrow.

Of unstained redwood I have framed it,
With many windows and a stone-laid patio
Enclosing an almond tree and the broad leaves of the fig,
And over the roof the blades of the banana.

And there I sit alone and wait
While the rain falls cold and the sea is wrapped away.
The mud banks crumble, and the sleek banana leaves
Are blighted and tattered by the storm.

And will she come when the spring comes?
When the almond blossoms and the bees are in the
    sagebrush
And the sea is blue again where the canyon cuts
    the water? . . .
Will ever my belovèd come when the spring comes?

The Milk of the Desert

There was water among the mountains,
    for the sun was red
    on the snows of the summits
    and the live oaks were black in the canyons.

Here . . . men died
    for lack of water,
    and no cattle grazed
    upon cactus and greasewood.

But now they have stirred me
    with the blade of the colter
    and have slaked my thirst
    with gray snow-water.

They have planted trees
    to darken the sun for me
    with little circles of shadow
    slow-moving about the stem.

Ah sweet in the noonday
    the coolness of snow-water
    running between the rows
    and circling the stems of the orange trees!

Hibiscus

No one has seen me crying . . .
No one has seen me!

I know a hiding place behind the mountain
Up through the sagebrush and the spotted cactus.
Soon as I feel the rush of tears upon me
I slip away from the eyes of men and women
Swift as a mountain beast scurrying to cover.
And no one sees me.

Here by the seaside among the palms and roses,
I am a proverb for light step and laughter.
Every one knows me.
My teeth hold always a scarlet flower
Bitten from a branch of the roadway hibiscus.
And when the moon breaks through the eucalyptus,
Every one knows I dance till the morning
Wreathed and girdled with honeysuckle. . . .

Ah, no one has seen me!
Up behind the mountain in a savage canyon
Cactus rots and red mud powders.
No palm stirs a fronded shadow.
No one is there to make me flash my white teeth
And stand between me and my spell of crying!

The High Mountains

I

I will drive up my sheep to the high mountains
    following the snow.
There the grass is tender green in August,
    growing close,
Close-starred with little buttercups
    and with blue cyclamen.
There the waters never fail,
    and pussy willows
Late in summer shed the smell of April
    off budding sprays.

We will leave the rank voluptuous valleys,
    vine and olive,
Cattle fattened on alfalfa
    and milk-fed swine.
We will drive on past the hills scorched brown
    with passion of the sun,
Through the deep pine-shadowed canyons —
    never stopping
Till we reach the level of little rivers
    and great snows.

For my sheep have supple joints
    and sure feet
To seek and clamber over surfaces
    of risky granite,
And my sheep have heavy fleece
    against the cold.

II

I have made my bed upon the earth
between a pine tree and a boulder,
wrapping the darkness round me for a blanket.

No one knows where I have made my bed
in a secret place
in the dark.

    The brook is loud in the canyon
    under my hill,
    and through the stems of the pines
    I am aware of a presence
    steep and starlit.

    Certain dusky fir-tops,
    leaning together,
    silently confer,
    and the stars among them
    and above them
    benignly wait upon their counsels.

And that is the last I know
as I fall asleep
where I have made my bed in the dark
between a pine tree and a boulder.

III

Pine boughs are friendly
    overhead,
Spreading out their dusky
    many-fingered palms . . .

Through the open spaces
        the stars
Marching all night
        across our moveless shelter.

The pines are of our mortal birth,
        warmed by our sun,
Rooting by watercourses
        of our homely planet.
We rest upon their needles
        that are of our own clay.

This wind that fills our nostrils
        with clean forgetfulness
Is bred of airs that warm and cool
        along our waters.
Close to the earth
        its currents flow,
The sweet familiars of the valleys
        where we lie.

Close to the earth
        we lie,
Content to feel the firm resistance
        of her bosom,
And fatherly shelter
        of our own pines.

And yet before we sleep
        we love to catch
At the black edge of a crag
        the glint of a star,
Or splintering its rays
        on the pine needles.

IV

    Here on the high plateau
        the woods are thinner
And the stars may not be
        kept away.

No foot of mountain flower,
        however daring,
Can scale these toothed and pyramided
        peaks —
Defying even the snow
        to make a lodgment.

Even the snow in the clefts
        is earth-born,
Sucked from the life-infested ocean —
        sweet water-mist —
To be released again as sweet
        life-giving water.

But the peaks above it, bleak
        as dead moons,
Hold commerce only
        with the starry region,
Owning no kinship to things
        mortal . . .

Here on the high plateau
        the woods are thinner
And the stars may not be
        kept away.

V

"Mine is the obstinate enterprise
    of tortured pines
Rooting between the boulders
    amid August snows,
And the serene endurance
    of granite summits
That have survived an age
    of grinding ice.
Upon my flinty ridges
    rests the glow of evening
    and of morning,
And the long white clear light
    of nights and days
    without event."

VI

"The blue cut in the toothed divide,
    blue fathomless distance cutting down
    into dazzle of snow.

"High above the deep-cleft canyon,
    high above even the stoical pine-tops,
    among things only hard and cold,

"How should this bring to mind
    the sandy reaches of soft Coronado?" . . .
    O heart! O doves and palms and roses!

VII

All night beneath pines
    the sound of waters pouring,
    pouring from hidden springs
    in the many-channeled mountains.

At dawn the perfect hush
   at the end of all trails
   where snow lies cold
   in its most secret fastness.

Westward the sun is warm
   far across snow-laid ranges,
   but here in the great cirque,
   in the dimness of twilight,

Gray barren crags,
   scored and ancient faces,
   presiding in solemn silence
   over the birth of waters.

Dead granite raised aloft
   behind the wooded canyons
   where no tracks nor voices
   betray the presence of life.

Cold themselves and barren,
   foster mothers of life,
   gray heads consulting together
   about the cradle.

THE LIFE WE IMAGE

..."Gaining as we give
The life we image, even as I do now."

Living Room

There will be laughter in this room and kissing,
And every chair will be the starting place
For thoughts that take on words and boldly face
Ultimate questions, hitting square and missing,
Gamesome and grave. There will be scorn and hissing
For all that pharisees and fools embrace.
There will be kindly wit and courtly grace. . . .
There will be laughter in this room and kissing.

When we are gone . . . O death! . . . there will have been
These things which no oblivion shall rub out
While here the very chairs and tables shout
Of all these happy walls have heard and seen.
In space too packed with living done for grieving
Where shall the hateful spider start his weaving?

Winter Night

We are a houseful for a bitter night
To bark at. For, besides the watchful keepers,
Mother and father, and two fisty sleepers
Dreaming of Sea-hawk, Sindbad, fear and fight,
The twelve white mice together are a sight
When they have shut in sleep their little peepers,
And in her basket, with her furry creepers
Tucked under, sleeps the kitten snug and tight.

We trust that Christianson has heaped the fire
For ten below, and so our Christmas tree,
Protected from the blizzard winds that rock
Her sisters, glimmering in her fine attire,
May stand all night and listen cosily
To the low prattle of the kitchen clock.

Perennial

It is a marvel how this Christmas tree,
Year after year, as sure as comes December
And snow, should so infallibly remember
To spring up in this corner and to be
Laden with bells and candles handsomely.
We have great need of these since the last ember
Of summer cheer has died out in November
And the heart craves comfort and mystery.

Our Christmas tree comes when the world is coldest,
And all these bells and candles are a reason
Drawing the clan together for a season,
Rejoicing, from the youngest to the oldest,
To warm our hands and hearts and make us bold
To face the world again and fight the cold.

Swan Maiden

People who keep a swan maiden must cherish
And tend her ever with distinguished care,
Never address her in a manner bearish
And rough, nor fail to stroke her sea-green hair.
For though she may be very fond of childer
And full of merriment and tenderness,
One churlish word might suddenly bewilder
And send her looking for that feather dress.

When after dinner we are set to playing
At cards, before an open fire toasting,
And all the world is rollicking and boasting . . .
Oh see! across her mouth that strange look straying!
She will be dreaming — or it is my notion —
Of white swans sailing on a wide green ocean.

Blood Is Thicker than Water

I have seven sons, and they are blithe and hale,
That ride all day to hunt the stag and bear.
Come night, we feast and fling a jibe to care
Over our smoking meats and foaming ale.
And each will touch the harp and weave a veil
Of cunning sound about some debonair
And brave old story — be it Guenevér
Or the strange hunting of the Holy Grail.

We seek no quarrel upon any man,
But rouse us and you rouse the tiger's brood.
These all are brothers and my flesh and blood,
Certain of this, that I would give my span
Of life to save one son from agony —
As I am certain all would die for me.

Affinities

(IN MEMORIAM H. R.)

There is a Jew in whom I take delight
More than in any man uncircumcized,
For he is proud as one that is baptized
And gentle as a blushing acolyte.
Truth is the game he tracks both day and night,
Knowing how seldom truth may be surprised.
That is a man I'd trust with all I prized
Most dear — my sons, my honor, and my right.

And when we turn together from the sham
And shoddy of the earth to heaven's gate,
There if the holy Peter think to slam
His portals in our faces with a damn,
We shall go up together and in state
Into the house of holy Abraham.

Cave Talk

What are you doing there by the shore?
  —I'm pushing out my boat.
I mean to follow the sun across
    To islands far remote.
It may be I shall find a land
    Where fruits and spices grow;
Fairer women, stronger men,
    And mountains topped with snow.

—Nay, go not forth across the wave,
    Where ghosts and monsters be.
What fairer folk can heart desire
    Than my sweet cubs and me?
And who shall bring us fish and flesh
    When you are gone away?
Come, spread the net and string the bow —
    But fare not far astray!

What are you scratching there on the rock?
  —I'm carving pictures here,
Feathered bird and otter furred,
    To bide for many a year.
When a thousand moons have waxed and waned
    And I am dust and smoke,
Men shall behold my handiwork
    And praise the master-stroke.

—O sluggard, leave your idle ways.
    Behold our bitter dearth!
We shiver in the frosty wind
    And couch upon the earth.
Go, strip the otter and her cubs
    For coats and kirtles fine,
And pluck the feathered bird to strew
    A bed for me and mine.

What are you doing out in the dark?
　—I count the stars in the sky,
And wonder if they are the souls
　Of such as you and I;
And if the bear and the lean gray wolf
　Have souls like yours and mine,
That go to feed the milky way
　Or make the great stars shine.

—O dreamer, what are the stars to you
　And the souls of wolf and bear?
The gray wolf prowls about the rock
　And sniffs upon the air;
His eyes are shining in the dark
　Like stars above the sea!
Build high the fire before the cave
　To guard my cubs and me.

What do you see that stare so hard?
　—A face all smooth and white,
And breasts and shoulders smooth and round
　And soft in the flickering light.
I muse how wondrous women are
　And how unlike to men . . .
I saw white arms in the sea at dawn . . .
　Long since . . . and never again . . .

—You love me not, O stranger man,
　Who talk of women and men,
Of white arms in the sea at dawn . . .
　You love me never again!
You sit and dream the while I wait—
　And the little ones all asleep . . .
Oh, if you love me a little, man,
　Kiss me . . . or I shall weep!

The View at Gunderson's

Sitting in his rocker waiting for your tea,
Gazing from his window, this is what you see:

A cat that snaps at flies; a track leading down
By log-built shanties gray and brown;

The corner of a barn, and tangled lines of fence
Of rough-hewn pickets standing dense;

The ghost of a tree on a dull, wet day;
And the blanket fog where lies the bay.

But when he's seen the last of you,
Sitting in his rocker, what's *his* view?

(For there he sits, day in day out,
Nursing his leg — and his dreams, no doubt.)

The snow-slide up behind the *gaard;*
The farm beside old Trondhjem fjord;

Daughters seven with their cold blue eyes,
And the great pine where his father lies;

The boat that brought him over the sea;
And the toothless woman who makes his tea.

(Their picture, framed on the rough log wall,
Proves she had teeth when he was tall.)

He sees the balsam thick on the hill
And all he's cleared with a stubborn will.

And last he sees the full-grown son
For whom he hoards what he has won.

You saw little worth the strife:
What he sees is one man's life.

The Dance in the Steerage

The lights are dim on the steerage deck,
    But the stars are big and nigh,
And a white wave flashes by the rail
    Whenever the deck goes high.

They have cleared a space among the ropes
    Enough to spin a top,
And there the cook and a mother of nine
    Spin round with never a stop —

Spin like a top, spin like a ball,
    Spin like a humming wheel,
Spin like a world upon its poles
    On tireless toe and heel.

And what's the tune to which they spin?
    Accordion, fiddle, flute?
Tune of the white wave, tune of the stars,
    Tune of the great souls mute?

Never a word and never a smile
    And never a glance they drop,
Never a pause to scrape and bow,
    But round and round like a top.

Never a glance and never a word
    And never the ghost of a smile,
While stars go marching down the west
    And waves wash mile on mile.

And is it love? And is it prayer?
    And is it childish glee?
It is the craving of the world
    And that which had to be.

Swanhild

Must we needs pity her, we that remain,
That have not tasted the sharpness of pain?

Strings that utter response so low
And dead to the passionate strokes of the bow

Pity a spirit strung so taut
To the grief we shunned and the joy she sought?

Joy she sought and the grief we dread
Are throbbing strings to wake the dead.

Joy she missed, and grief she found
So sharp it drove her under the ground.

But her pain it rang out clear and high —
And our best note is a toneless sigh!

Success Story

    I have both eaten when I was not hungry
        And have gone empty when my soul craved meat.
    I have spent nights and days with those I loved not,
        Sundered for life from those I found most sweet.
    I have reaped many a crop not worth the sowing,
        Leaving unsown what was my finest seed. . . .
    And now I am grown fat and full of honors,
        I shall sleep soft . . . until I sleep indeed!

Salute

Press wormwood and all bitter weeds,
You hypocrites and pharisees,
And mix a drink as sour and wry
As your own barren hearts and creeds,

And I will take and drink it up
And gather strength with every drop,
And drink a health to all your tribe
And thank you for the bitter cup.

But pour the blood of grapes and figs
And sweeten with your canting lies . . .
I'll take the drink and say a grace,
And chuck it in your dirty face!

Love in Ambush

When first the dreary news she told,
   His look returned her mute dismay.
   The winter prospect, gray on gray,
Showed not a hint of green or gold.

Before love passed, his will was done:
   Another heart began to beat,
   The paths were laid for other feet,
And other eyes must greet the sun.

This was the worst they had to face:
   For as they gazed, each one must think,
   Now of their chain the utmost link
Was fixed and twisted into place.
  . . . .

But day by day a change appears
   As dull misgiving yields to hope.
   The woman gives her fancy scope,
The man wears out his wilder fears.

She in her girl the gifts may gain
   She did in vain for self beseech;
   What he has sought and failed to reach
He in his boy may now attain.

So while their hopes together range,
   Their eyes on one another fall
   To find the fashioner of all
Has worked a transformation strange.

Love, whom they thought to have beguiled
   To be their slave and summer sport,
   Has tricked them in such wondrous sort
They are his captives . . . reconciled!

Christmas Trees

The dusky children of the wood
We catch them and imprison them.
We set them where the cradle stood
And gorgeously bedizen them.

We load them down with ropes of pearls
Like little captive princesses
And circle round with boys and girls
The sisters of the silences.

Their brothers underneath the moon
With snow upon their shoulders sleep
And break with never a shout nor croon
The silence which the boulders keep.

But these within the house of toys
Behold a little wearily
The antics of the girls and boys
That sport and carol cheerily.

They stand like strangers at the feast,
But patiently and graciously
As if their souls had never ceased
To dream and ponder spaciously.

The Black Land

    I will plow the land,
Turning up the black soil.
I will ride upon this heaving surface
As a boat rides upon the water.
Even as a boat
Cleaving the water with an eager keel,
I have run a furrow
Straight across the ridges.

    I will sow down this field,
Scattering gems.
With both hands will I scatter
Quivering emeralds out of a bottomless pouch.

    As I tread the loam
My feet sink deep.
The black earth embraces my ankles
And clings to my bent knees.
    I sing as I go
Scattering emeralds.
The wind sings upon my lips,
And pearls stream off my neck and forehead.
I am bathed in a sweat of pearls.

    Eyes straight forward
Rest on a brightening ultimate slope.

Succession

    It is not as if I stood alone.
When I stop to rest the horses
And take a look at the sky,
It is not me
So much as my father
Stopping in the same furrow:
For I have his shoulders
And his eyes.

    And when I stumped that field,
I felt as if I were his father,
Who cleared the first land
And built the house.
My father built on the ell,
But he slept himself
In his father's bed
In the old house;
And that's where I sleep.

    I hope my son will stick to the land.
I like to watch him plow
Upon that hillside,
And burn brush
Along the road.
It is as much me
As it is himself,
And as much my father
As either of us.

The Red Land

In the autumn,
Bathed in gold dust,
I shall strip the red land
Of a golden harvest.

Oh, fruitful as the red land
Bearing golden harvest
In the autumn,
Bountiful as the prairie
Heaving milky breasts
On flushed horizons!

My hand slackens
In the act of cutting,
While I lose myself
In these blue distances.

The scythe pauses
On the neck of the wheat
As my heart faints against
These flushed horizons.

I that have seen the sky,
In the time of reaping,
Between her breasts
In the wheat field,
Sowing and reaping,
There I worship
The land!

Songs for Dagmar

II

Now gleam the candles down the board, high raised on crystal stems like fluttering blossoms. Doors swing softly as, without faltering, the appointed dinner makes its slow, deliberate progress. Now in the dusk gleam shoulders, and about mouths and eyes of men and women flutter smiles, while up and down the board flashes the fire of gaiety and speculation.

I know that you are there, my dear, soft-voiced, slow-syllabled, beyond the roses and azaleas. I hear the falling of your voice like water upon water. I listen for your laugh, which is like the wind's in the poplar, and for your long silence, like the silence of the pinewood. And I am busy too, paying the minted coin of thought and friendship.

O know you not, my love, that I am here as in your presence? Send me a glance across the heaped azaleas. Send me a glance to let me know you know me conscious of you beyond the roses, merry with these, but always in your presence.

V

Round about our vineyard prowl the wolves. Red eyes, starved bellies howl and yap on us that pasture among the vines. Slavering muzzles, quivering paws, the prowlers, forward rushing, falling back, tearing the earth, running round in a ring. They that find no flesh to fill their bellies, how they hate us that feed on the golden and purple grapes!

Fear not, companion, fear not these! Only keep burning the fire on the altar. How they fear the fire! Behold them baffled, shivering like whipped dogs, slinking back in the shadow, back to the place of tombs, slinking among the fallen slabs and the broken pillars. Hear them whining! Hear them barking, with hunger and malice, with fear and hate.

Fear no wolves, O you that feed with me together upon the golden and purple grapes! Only bring spices, clove and myrrh and spikenard. Sprinkle over the flame. Let it leap high and clear, let it burn steady through all nights upon the altar!

MINNEAPOLIS SKYLINES
1915

The Chimneys

Now the dusk settles over river and city,
Dim, rolling vapors rise to meet the crawling,
Heavy breath of the chimneys brown and murky,
And joining forces in the deepening twilight,
They make advance in one dark, ghostly tide.
Already it has filled the river-bottoms,
And steadily rises round the spindling legs
Of the airy bridges, till they are overwhelmed.
Now vanish gable, spire, and all that pictures
Our human life and labor along the skies.
The fog has drawn its smutty finger across
The clear gold of the fading sunset. Only,
As lone survivors of the submerged city,
Four slender shafts rise black upon the gold,
Piercing the smother: idle as in a dream,
Four clustered smokestacks. Having clean forgotten
Their daily toil, with what serene detachment
They lift their nostrils in the golden air,
As if they had no part nor interest
In the cloudy fortunes of the world below!

Power

Moveless he stands against the iron railing,
With all the world about him in commotion.
The mighty water races on beneath him
To storm the falls. From the unnumbered chimneys
Flutters the smoke in long wind-shredded pennons.
The switching engines, blowing clouds of steam,
Tear back and forth, while over its granite arches
Thunders the night express, steady as fate,
With pomp of banners and proud illumination.
On every hand is power visible,
And yonder where the mills and powerhouses
Are lighting up their tier on tier of windows
Intenser it moves in spinning shaft and wheel,
Or lurks disguised in sleek and humming turbines.
Yet in that quiet figure by the railing,
Frail as a wisp between the sky and water,
Labors the sovereign force of all the planet.
Master of all the powers of earth and air,
He well may gaze upon his harnessed river
And stand unmoved amidst the hurly-burly.

Milwaukee Depot

Impatiently he paces to and fro
Along the platform, peering anxiously
Down the dark tunnel of the hooded shelter
Out on the switching yards. There breeds confusion
Among the tangled tracks this winter morning.
Red lanterns swing from agitated arms
Of unseen semaphores, and frosty stretches
Of ties and rails take form and straightway vanish.
Hither and thither run the barking engines
Without an aim, wrapt in their own white breath,
And through the volumed, ever-shifting vapors
Loom spectral and uncertain the gray masses
Of mills and elevators. Out of a world
So strange, bewildering and phantasmagoric,
He scarcely can believe his train will come,
Radiant and sure at the appointed moment,
Finding its way from that far-distant city
Through the dim, unimagined wildernesses —
And she, whose missive flutters in his fingers,
Shall stand before him there and smile upon him!

Bohemian Flats

One side the river burrows deep beneath
The wooded cliffs with ragged stone outcroppings.
The other side it shuns the ancient banks
And so embraces in its curving elbow
A little flock of low-roofed huts that nestle
About the feet of the great straddling bridges.
How far below they lie, like some enchanted
Town in the weedy hollows of the ocean!
The cottonwoods that wave their lofty plumes
Above the ridgepole creep along the bottoms,
And even the wooden spire that herds the faithful
From end to end of the village, reaching upward,
Rests in the shadow of the railway trestles.
Those that speed past above by train or trolley
Are unaware of a world that lies beneath them.
And the glaring light of the lamps that swing on high
Falls dim and dreamlike on the sunken village,
Strained through fathoms of fog that lie above it.
No rumor comes to us aloft. They seem
Buried away beneath the care and fever
Of our insatiate struggle, as we fancy
Some sleepy village in a mountain valley
Ages and ages past, and far away.

Urban Colloquy

At midnight, turning sharply round a corner,
I met a vision: high in the air there hung,
Between the looming banks of the narrow street,
Two shining faces, whose exalted orbs
Seemed to dispute the regency of heaven.
One was the moon's and one the old clock-tower's.
The clock's face looked the ruddier and the rounder.
And yet I seemed to hear the pale moon mutter:
"It was not always thus. 'Tis scarce ten decades
Since I, that looked on swarming Nineveh,
Peered down the long stems of the Norway pine
Where now this rival flouts me; and for mortals,
These shores were peopled with gray wolves and gophers."
And if the clock replied, "Mile upon mile
No sign of aught but human habitation,"
The surly moon made answer, "Ay, but wait!"

PARISIAN DRYPOINTS
1913

Pont Royal

Still dripped the sycamores along the quays,
And the whole sky was black save where, above
The long black bulk of the Louvre, smouldered and glowed
The nightly reflex of the boulevards.
The river flowed more dark for the bordering lights
Doubled and twisted in its troubled deeps,
And everywhere along the quays and across
The span of the bridges, silent and darkly massed,
The people of Paris watched their spectacle.

High over the crouching mass of the Island-City
The blank sky blossoms into flowers of fire,
Trailing across the darkness like a trellis—
Ragged chrysanthemums of heartening gold
With twisting petals that stretch to the limit of vision,
And tenuous violet sprays of wistaria, swaying,
Drooping and vanishing in the glooms of the City.

Yonder the battlements of the ancient prison
Brighten a moment and sink upon deeper gloom.
Now plays the light round the delicate spire of the Chapel.
And the murky, age-worn towers of Notre Dame
Like mouldering granite cliffs by a stormy ocean
Stand out in the raining spray of gold and silver,
With base submerged in the bottomless deeps of shadow.
Up from the bed of the river a fiery fountain
Ceaselessly plays from under the roots of the bridges,
While dark the massive arches loom and speak
Of the age-long, tireless feet of eager pilgrims.
Now off to the right round the dome of the Institute
The brightness hovers, conjuring up for an instant
The laurelled peerage whose unresting spirits
Are lightnings in the gulfs of human blindness.

And thus across the blank face of the sky
Was Paris writing out her latest credo,
The vision of her thinkers and her dreamers,
For whom the course of the world through cycles of ages,
The blooming and drooping of life on the stems of the planets,
Are seen as play of a jubilant fount unceasing,
Living fountain of light ever rising and falling,
With bursts and trails of vivid and joyous splendor,
Across the blind and speechless face of the night.

Quai Voltaire

Crisply above her head the broad leaves rustled,
Vividly bright below but roofed with darkness,
And bright the rare drops fell in the freshening breeze.
She paid no heed to wind nor rain, but rested
Quiet upon her perch on the parapet
With hands clasped tight between her clinging knees.
Her cheeks in the gaslight shone all fresh and cool.
One way she gazed intent, the way all faces
Were turned but mine. No smile disturbed her features.
Only whenever her face glowed with the splendor
Whereon she looked her brightening eyes betrayed
The thoughtless joy that held her there enchanted.
If ever human heart or brain be vacant,
It was her boon at that surpassing moment.
I stood and watched her and she paid no heed.

Rue de Seine

Here where one narrow street of towering fronts
Cuts through another, peering down behold
A scene of strange and sleepy animation.
No wheels nor hooves may touch that tawny pavement
During the days of fête, but toes and heels
Of those that house behind the eyeless shutters
Possess alone its brown and slippery surface.
Upon their platform near the sausage-seller's
Fiddle and horn compound the rude enchantment
Wherein these shabby toes and heels are tangled,
And on each corner, from its dim café,
Tables and chairs across the sidewalk sprawling
Reach to the gutter. Here the lookers-on
Consume in silence their Lethean syrups.
Through all the days of fête it is tradition
To smile upon the votaries of pleasure
And so reflect a moiety of joy.
And the dim figures in the hovering mist,
Between the showers do but follow custom,
Turning and turning on the slippery pavement
And grinding out the dingy meal of pleasure.
The cabbage-sellers of the Rue de Buci,
The canvas-daubers of the Rue Saints-Pères—
Some have been fed today and some are fasting—
And convalescents and young cut-cadavers,
And youth and middle age all undistinguished,
Dimmer and dimmer in the deepening murk,
Like creatures at the bottom of a well.

Saint Germain des Prés

When first I took my chosen place commanding
The long gray vista of the boulevard,
All faces formed a dense and eager circle
About the little shadowed isle of pavement
Where the red-shirted tumblers do their marvels.
It is a sport Boccaccio and Villon
Loved well, and through the misty drift of years
It has not failed to cheat life of much sorrow
In all the cities where men follow joy.
A moment later the whole scene is shifted,
All heads are backward thrown, and the whole street
Is like one finger pointing where that bird
Slides smoothly down the white slope of the sky,
Hovers a moment round the craggy tower
Of the old gray church, and passes out of sight.
And as they gaze these childlike faces lighten
As if it were some star-in-the-east that sheds
Its hopeful visionary brightness on them:
While here at the door even our staid patronne
Fluttering in and out with many a glance
At the heavenly wonder smiles and smiles upon us,
As if to say, "Is not dear life amusing?"

Folies-Bergère

She whom you find so cold and inexpressive —
Even to her lover a fireless Artemis —
Could you behold her once before the footlights
Would dazzle and transport with passion feigned.
Between her dressing-glass and the waiting wings
Is worked a change mysterious as the emergence
From its shroud of the gold and azure butterfly.
Hovering there before the shadowy curtains
She blossoms and she flames in light and motion.
Her dancing is the eloquence of a love
That pays no tribute to confining life.
Life is a dull and weary way, but the dance
A flower as rare as the sky-rooted orchis,
With scent to drown the memory of the real.

Café d'Harcourt

He sits established underneath his awning
Before the lighted window, like a Buddha
Snugly enshrined within a jeweled casket.
His narrow eyes and grinning parchment visage
Proclaim him of the race antipodal
Who make the most of Buddhas, and to all
Your courteous inquiries he makes answer
In French of Tientsin: "I am of China."
Perhaps the seed of emperors, and come
To learn the mysteries of government,
He will return to take the helm of empire,
A pregnant orator — at least a statesman.
But though you ply him with a thousand questions,
And though he shows no sign of failing patience
But ever seems most eager to oblige you,
You get no further in your quest of knowledge,
And must digest one statement comprehensive
In oriental French: "I am of China."
You think you might have known that without asking.

Café Steinbach

One who has languished in Siberian prisons
And mined for golden learning in Toulouse,
For marketing perchance in Buenos Aires,
Now takes his summer ease in idle Paris
With comrades of the hospitable Quarter,
Who rise at noon, and dine not long ere daybreak
Under the care of Maurice at the Steinbach.
On no man's forehead can you read his fate,
So intervolved is circumstance, but here
Is written out so much of one man's nature,
Frank loving-kindness and good-fellowship.
And by his words you learn that he has pondered
The lore of books and puzzling map of life.
For while the women, with their pocket-mirrors
And powder-puffs and napkins, make an effort
To freshen up their tarnished visages,
And Maurice dodges featly here and there
With steaming platters and with pleasantries,
And while the dancers thread the crowded tables,
Sluggishly whirling like the muddy current
Among the weedy rocks of some back-water,
And the card-players go on undiverted,
This Russian youth holds grave and steady converse
Of Marx and Plato, Washington and Ruskin,
Of government and misery and crime,
Humanity, and of the Golden Age.

Boulevard Clichy

She has sat long before her glass half-drained.
The bright café is very near deserted
This rainy midnight, and it is not merry.
Once more she readjusts her limp aigrette
That has done service on so many faces,
And some less fresh and winning than her own.
And yet none comes however she may linger!
Her muddy slippers are well tucked away
Beneath the table — slippers that at midday
She cleaned and blacked in her own attic chamber
Seated upon the floor beside her pallet.
But many ways have been traversed in vain.
By this I see hers is a merchandise
Of little estimation. She whose traffic
Is joy and pleasure has not even dined.
And gaiety is very hard to compass
When you have love for sale and none will buy.

Rue Bonaparte

You that but seek your modest rolls and coffee,
When you have passed the bar, and have saluted
Its watchful madam, then pray enter softly
The inner chamber, even as one who treads
The haunts of mating birds, and watch discreetly
Over your paper's edge. There in the corner,
Obscure, ensconced behind the uncovered table,
A man and woman keep their silent tryst.
Outside the morning floods the pavement sweetly;
Yonder aloft a maid throws back the shutters;
The hucksters utter modulated cries
As wistful as some old pathetic ballad.
Within, the brooding lovers, unaware,
Sit quiet hand in hand, or in low whispers
Communicate a more articulate love.
Sometimes she plays with strings and, gently leaning
Against his shoulder, shows him childish tricks.
She has not touched the glass of milk before her,
Her breakfast and the price of their admittance.
She has a look devoted and confiding
And might be pretty were not life so hard.
But he, gaunt as his rusty bicycle
That stands against the table, and with features
So drawn and stark, has only futile strength.
The love they cherish in this stolen meeting
Through all the day that follows makes her sweeter,
And him perhaps it only leaves more bitter.
But you that have not love at all, old men
That warm your fingers by this fire, discreetly
Play out your morning game of dominoes.

Parc Monceau

We were so happy in our pleasant gardens
This warm and gentle Sunday afternoon!
And all the world was there, seated at ease
Or strolling along the shaded walks — workmen
With folded hands, women with their workbaskets,
And capped and aproned nursemaids with their babies.
And some were silent, some playing games, and many
Quietly and with comfortable relish
Discoursed of Prussia and the coming struggle.
The sycamores bore high their lustrous crowns
And the willows trailed in the water where its quiet
Mirrors the columns white in semicircle
Of the ruined temple, haunt of loves and graces.
Massenet came in snatches to our ears
Like the sunlight sifted through the leafy roof.
Then suddenly the air grew thick and heavy
And sunlight failed as clouds drew rapidly
Across the sky their chill asbestos curtain,
And before we knew it we were making haste —
With forward leaning bodies and huddled skirts
And slanting fury of raindrops at our heels —
Down graveled paths and over grassy lawns
For awninged harbor of cafés and doorways
Or pell mell down the yawning throat of the subway.
We were too well accustomed to such usage
To make complaint, but yet we felt like children
Crossed in their hopes by inscrutable caprice
Of grownups. Heaven smiled, and heaven frowned,
And put an end to one more holiday.

Quai d'Orsay

What children dance by night in Paris gardens?

Black water long has slipped beneath the bridges.
Down the wide alleys of the Tuileries
The nightly urgent drummer-boy has passed
And the tall guardians of the public walks
Have driven home the lovers and loiterers
This fresh and eager night of June. O June!
Your chestnuts and your poplars and your lindens,
Your broad-leaved sycamores with mottled boles,
Your ivy and your tall aspiring lilacs
Have put on all their green. It is the fête
Of summer madness up and down the city.
Yet was I not prepared for such a vision
In midmost Paris, near the hour of midnight.

Through the barred gateway of this high-walled garden,
Discreet behind its proud hôtel, behold
A scene of mild and summer-golden radiance
Such as an airy child's heart might imagine
Along the floor of rosy summer clouds.
And it is sure no paradise imagined
To those who foot it lightly down the pathways
Threading geranium beds and heliotrope.
For while their happy little feet all bare
Deliciously reject the moistened gravel
Or linger a moment on the grassy borders,
And forward bound to strains of hidden music,
They are no longer little girls in Paris,
But charioteers and mettled steeds careering

Along the sunny arch of noonday heaven,
Or now, with shifting lights upon them falling
And play of waving veils and sinuous motion,
Waters and winds and planetary bodies.
As when the earth, blocking the radiant sun,
Shoots into space its spectral cone of shadow,
And the bright face of the moon darkens and saddens,
So falls the dusk upon these fluttering fleeces —
For but an instant — and the moment after
Falls the dazzle of light upon the ocean,
Welter of green and orange, blue and silver:
And ever the circling motion of steady planets
That wheel their orbits round the suns that bore them,
Girdled themselves with moons and phosphorescence.

And yet these are but little girls in Paris,
In midmost Paris, near the hour of midnight. . . .
What little girls? and whence? . . . a throng of questions . . .
And whither from this garden to emerge,
From this enchantment into disenchantment?
Whose children? For she cannot be their mother
Who guides their motions in her foreign speech,
Her brisk and uncaressing English tongue,
Nor he the father who, in shrill Parisian,
Commands the shift of lights upon the dancing,
And from his balcony surveys the stage,
Reckoning up for sure his future profits.
From many firesides have they been gathered,
From hearths where now the fire is extinguished,
Or hearths where never any fire was lighted.
How many griefs and shames lurk in the shadow
For every sparkle of laughter in the light!

Our questions rest unanswered. Backward peering,
Merciful darkness greets us, and pitiful darkness
Forward, as this illumined garden stands
Rounded with dusky Paris, and as life
Upon our short-lived planet sparkles and glows
Among the soundless glooms of eternity.
Only this night of June we hear the voices
And the fresh laughter of the witless children,
And among all the riddles this is certain
That children dance tonight in Paris gardens.

Acknowledgments

Acknowledgment is made for permission to reprint certain poems first published elsewhere, as follows: *The American Mercury,* Cyprian Hymn; *Poetry: A Magazine of Verse,* Cave Talk, The View at Gunderson's, The Black Land, Succession, The Red Land, Rue Bonaparte; *The Bellman,* The Dance in the Steerage; *The Atlantic Monthly,* Urban Colloquy, Café d'Harcourt, Café Steinbach, Quai d'Orsay; *The Survey,* The Chimneys, Power; *The Forum,* Pont Royal (courtesy of Events Publishing Company).

J. W. B.